Valerie Dignam was born and grew up in Dublin, Ireland. She moved to Jersey when she was 19 years old and soon discovered it would make a perfect base for her many journeys. It was here she developed the travel bug. She now lives back in Ireland in County Wicklow with her husband. This is her first book.

To Paul, my husband and backpacker companion, and to my daughter, Claire, for her constant encouragement.

In memory of my parents, Edward and Monica.

Valerie Dignam

ON THE HIPPY TRAIL
TO INDIA

AUSTIN MACAULEY PUBLISHERS™

LONDON • CAMBRIDGE • NEW YORK • SHARJAH

A CIP catalogue record for this title is available from the British Library.

ISBN 9781035818624 (Paperback)
ISBN 9781035818631 (ePub e-book)

www.austinmacauley.com

First Published 2024
Austin Macauley Publishers Ltd®
1 Canada Square
Canary Wharf
London
E14 5AA

I would not have undertaken this journey without Paul, my adventurous companion at the time who agreed to join me on our overland trip to India. And of course, the journey was made all the more memorable with the great group of people travelling with us on the Budget Bus. I am grateful for having had the opportunity to meet them all and share that special time.

Thanks to Claire Dignam for the inspiration for the book cover design.

Preface

The story that follows is a combination of memories stored away in my head for over 40 years and a collection of dusty notes and old diaries retrieved from boxes that somehow survived our many house moves. Here, I will attempt to bring them together again and relive a journey overland on the Hippy trail to India in 1976.

I was inspired to write my account of our journey when I found myself with more than enough spare time during the pandemic when I, along with people worldwide, found ourselves in lockdown. It was the perfect opportunity to bring my story to life. The 2020/2021 pandemic had turned lives upside down in every corner of the globe. We are now in our third lockdown and slowly unwinding back to freedom. It has been difficult at times, but it has also been a time of reflection for me and everyone affected, with lengthy separations from loved ones, loss of loved ones, and adapting to living without the freedoms we took for granted over a year ago. For me, this trip reflects on a time of freedom when it was possible to travel overland from Europe to Asia in a carefree manner. The pleasure of meeting people from various countries and experiencing their cultures had a profound effect on my life and turned travel into the love of my life. Overland travel was unique in that it introduced us to each country gradually, as opposed to air travel where we land in an airport six hours after take-off and miss out on the special and wonderful experiences in between.

As I write this, I realise how precious that time was and how lucky we were to be able to just take off without a care in the world. Paul was my boyfriend at that time, luckily, he loved to travel and was a willing companion for the journey. He has been my backup memory bank, helping me draft this story. I hope it will be as much fun to read as it was to be there.

Let's Go!

In order to protect identities some names and details have been changed.

An advertisement in the Private Eye magazine planted the seed that would grow into our first big adventure. A one-way ticket overland to India would cost £80 with Budget Bus. Adventure was guaranteed. Budget Bus was based in London and set off from there, bringing curious travellers out East in search of new culture, spiritual guidance, and fun. It would certainly be a no-frills trip. The brochure was a little paper booklet stapled together with a yellow cover. Inside, it gave a brief description of what to expect during the six weeks it would take to cover 6,000 miles, and accommodation would be a mix of camping, hostels, or budget hotels when possible.

Camping shops were very rare back then in Jersey, where we lived at the time, so we had to order our camping gear from a catalogue received from Blacks of Greenock in Scotland.

We chose lightweight everything, mindful of the fact that we would be carrying everything on our backs for most of the trip. We sent off the money and waited for the kit to arrive, and when it did, reality kicked in and we had to go.

Arriving in London a few days before the departure date allowed us time to do some sightseeing before we left. We stayed at a campsite in Crystal Palace where we met some American backpackers. They had been to India and gave us some tips about their travels there; our evenings were spent swapping travel stories. We did touristy things in London to kill some time until at last, the day of departure arrived on 6th September 1976. It was a Monday, and I remember thinking, what a way to spend a Monday! We bought some non-perishable food supplies, rolls of film, and a travel log for taking notes on our trip. Then, we made our way to Totteridge Station to catch the bus! When we arrived, more people were hovering around with backpacks, looking just as anxious as us, waiting to board the adventure bus. We all started chatting, wondering what type of bus would turn up. When it arrived, we couldn't believe how luxurious it was, with ventilation controls and reclining seats! But alas, it was too good to be true. Upon arrival at Dover docks, we were transferred to the "real" bus to Delhi. It was a lavender Bedford banger! The driver convinced us it would get us there, so we all stepped aboard. Most of us were in our twenties, either couples or lone travellers. Some were only going as far as Istanbul, others as far as Tehran, but most of us were heading to Delhi to explore India and beyond. We had one thing in common: adventure. We didn't have a guidebook, but Evan, our driver, was our guide and mentor throughout the journey. I remember one thing he said loud and clear as we sat ready to drive onto the ferry for Dover: 'Don't wipe your noses on the curtains.' As we would realise later in our journey, we had to be prepared for the unexpected on our journey with sometimes long stretches of driving through the night without stops for many hours. It was exciting too because of all the countries we would travel through to get to India.

Europe

The ferry from Dover arrived in Zeebrugge, Belgium. We reached Belgium at night and travelled in darkness through the country, so we saw little of it on the motorway. Transit through Germany was much the same, stopping only to change money. That was it, really, except for some nice towns and villages. But for the most part, we drove on the Autobahn, which meant we had little interaction with the locals. From Germany, we entered Austria, arriving at the border late in the evening. Evan took us to a good camping site, and we pitched up there for the night. In the morning, we could appreciate the beautiful location we were in, with surrounding mountains, lush green countryside, and crisp mountain air. The green pastures were stunning. We stopped here for two nights and used up our food supplies bought back in London. We cooked up a meal at the campsite and had some fun and a few drinks with the others from the bus. Later that day, we went exploring near the camping site and came across an old monastery selling beers. You could pull your own pint and reuse your container. It was a novelty; we had never done this before and enjoyed it and the brief time we had in Austria. At first, I thought Germany and Austria were similar, but Austria was so much prettier with its snow-capped mountains. It was simply magical, with the backdrop of the mountain chalet houses with their overhanging roofs and balconies decorated with beautiful flowers. Evan informed us that the location we were in was where 'The Sound of Music' had been filmed.

We were ready to move on to Yugoslavia. At the time of our visit in 1976, Yugoslavia was ruled by Tito's Communist Party, with a constitution closely modelled on that of the Soviet Union. Yugoslavia during the 1970s was heavily in debt. The mood was gloomy as we travelled through the country, and any towns and villages we visited showed the hardships suffered by its people clearly. By the early 1980s, inflation had gone up by 60% every 6 months. No wonder people there looked weary and downtrodden. The drive through the countryside was not very exciting as the terrain was mainly flat, farming land growing crops such as maize, wheat, and watermelons. Our journey took us through Belgrade, the capital, which was not very nice at that time and perhaps a little dead. Yugoslavia was a country of contrasts back then; on one side of the road, you would see old Mercedes cars, and on the other side, a donkey and cart driven by a poor farmer. Many of the buildings looked unfinished. Yugoslavia was not as popular a tourist destination then as it is today. Police checked in-transit tourists regularly throughout the country. At the campsite, we each had to hand over our passports until departure. It was grotty with very few basic facilities and generally unwelcoming. It, too, was guarded by the local police. It was at this campsite that we first spotted a bus with 'Bradford to Lahore' emblazoned on the side. We were to come across this bus later in our journey when it failed to navigate a tricky bend on the road! One day at a grocery store, I received a sweet as change because they didn't have currency to give me. Travel through Yugoslavia was not very exciting, and our driver ensured our stay was short. He suggested we drive through the night for a quick exit, and everyone on the bus agreed to moving on to a more fun destination, Greece.

Exploring Kavala, Greece

Arriving in Greece was refreshing after Yugoslavia. It was warmer, brighter in every way, with whitewashed houses glowing in the sun, adorned with colourful flowers in pots on windowsills. The richly coloured Bougainvillea trailed the balconies. Another plus was the food; it was simply delicious. It was such a contrast from gloomy Yugoslavia. We travelled from the border through the city of Thessaloniki and on to Kavala for a few days to relax in the sun at a wonderful campsite by the beach, not far from town. The facilities were excellent (after Yugoslavia, anywhere would be luxurious), and we were all so happy to be there. The locals were so friendly, and we soon got to know many of them. The beach campsite was heavenly, and we made the most of every moment, dipping in and out of the sea. We all took the bus to town one evening and found a local taverna to eat, drink, and be merry. It was a bustling, lively place. Tables and chairs were taken out to make room for us. We were like children when we found out they also had a jukebox and took turns playing our favourite songs. The Greeks were fun and very welcoming. After our meal and several ouzos, the Greek dancing and plate smashing began. Sidney was the first one up to dance. We were all surprised as he was usually quiet, but on this night, the Greek music set him off. He was in great spirits, and Greek dancing came naturally to him, especially after the copious amounts of Retsina and Ouzo he consumed that evening. The villagers loved him; they circled around him, clapping and cheering him on! As we left the taverna, everyone shook hands with us, making us promise to return soon, which we did. Our first night in Greece was to be a memorable one. We spent most of our time in Kavala at the beachside campsite. The weather was extremely hot, and we made the most of the freedom from the bus for a short while.

We had a communal barbecue on our last night in Kavala. Everyone helped out preparing and cooking the food, arranging supplies of drinks. Bill, our other driver, played his guitar, and we had a great session until we ran out of songs to sing or fell asleep. It was a clear starry night, and the only light we had was from the moon. We managed to go swimming that night too, in the moonlight. It truly was the best night since we left London. By now, everyone on the bus was well acquainted, especially after the beach party in Kavala. The next morning, everyone reluctantly boarded the bus, sad to leave Greece but also in a delicate state after the party the night before.

Camping in Kavala, Northern Greece

Arriving at the Greek-Turkish border, there was a noticeable difference with the Greek border guards wearing bright white uniforms, fancy hats, and knee-length socks with red tassels. By contrast, the Turkish guards were a stern-looking lot, dressed in army fatigues, and they were quite unfriendly too. We had gotten used to the formalities taking a long time at borders, mainly because of busloads of people waiting to go through, and everything was done manually and handwritten. They stamped everything; in fact, they loved stamps and paperwork! Some stamps were very nice and would decorate a full page in our passports. Once we had our entry visas signed and stamped, we were on our way. Our bus was running low on fuel as we crossed this border, and it seemed impossible to find a petrol station. Driving around trying to find one during the hottest part of the day was no good, as everyone on the bus was baking. The bus had no air conditioning; air came in only when we opened all the windows, and when we did, the combination of warm air, dust, and pollution came pouring in! After a very long time driving around on a near-empty fuel tank, we found a garage on the outskirts of Istanbul, which happened to be close to a campsite. It was there that we spent our first night in Istanbul. Traffic in Istanbul was crazy, the driving was chaotic, hooting horns, and motorists paid little attention to changing traffic lights. Anything that had wheels, including carts being pulled along by a donkey or a horse, clamoured to get through the chaos.

Fresh the next day, we headed into Istanbul to check out hotels, if that is what you could call them. They were more like hostels, and the first one we encountered was not very encouraging because as we waited in reception, an American lady came running down the stairs shrieking,

"Don't stay here, I've been robbed." That was enough for us to return to the bus. Eventually, most of us checked into the same hotel as it seemed safer in numbers. Besides, we just wanted to drop our bags and get on with seeing Istanbul. It was a fascinating place where West meets East by crossing Bosphorus Sea. It looked and felt so different. The Blue Mosque and the Bazaar, one of the largest in the world back then, were on our list to see. Our time was limited, so we had to pack in as much as possible every day. Another place on our list was the Pudding Shop. We had heard so much about it, not just for the delicious puddings but also as a place for overlanders to meet, swap info and sell stuff, and find cheap bus trips within Turkey or into Iran. Turkish food was so exotic to us, and we enjoyed the eastern spicy dishes and loved mealtimes!

The Bazaar in Istanbul was a gigantic bustling place full of colour and certainly the biggest market I had ever seen. Everything imaginable could be bought there, including spices, fruit, vegetables, cooked food, embroidered clothes, and some items I could not identify! It teemed with life. The aroma in the air of exotic spices made it all the more attractive. It was especially enchanting at night-time, with the blend of Turkish music and the colourful lights luring you further into its depths. Once you stepped in, it was difficult to find your way out. Stalls and shops intermingled and spilled into the streets, selling all sorts of colourful clothing, unusual items, and jewellery. The vendors worked hard at tempting you in for green tea or to smoke the Turkish Water Pipe, with a promise of no pressure if you only wanted to look. The trouble was, if you did find anything and asked the price, you immediately set the haggling situation in motion. It could take anything up to one hour to complete! The vendor didn't care how long it took, as long as he extracted your cash. We were new to all this and found it fun. One day, we were drawn into haggling for an Onyx Chess set, initially "just looking." It was beautiful but weighed a ton! The shop owner started with a crazy high price, then dropped to half his price. Even at that point, we still believed we were being ripped off. Negotiations always involved tea, a lot of tea, and what seemed like hours of bargaining. A fair price was reached, only for us to decide not to buy. The fun had worn off, and we were relieved to wriggle out of buying it. The shop owner wasn't happy, but we parted as friends. A lesson was learned, and from then on, we were careful about "just looking."

The Blue Mosque, Istanbul

Back at the hotel, there was a commotion between Sidney and the hotel manager. The offending items were a matchbox of bed bugs smothered in DDT (a powder for killing the bugs).

Sidney took them to the hotel manager to complain, but the guy just shrugged. Sidney refused to use the bed again. Instead, he slept on the floor in his sleeping bag and negotiated a cheaper nightly rate for the inconvenience. Sidney had worked as a teacher in the UK prior to embarking on this journey. He was also very fit and conscious of taking his daily vitamins, and he was particularly fussy about hygiene. Unfortunately, many of the establishments we encountered would not be very hygienic, which proved to be a major obstacle for Sidney. Nevertheless, he was a great character, and we loved having him as company on the bus journey.

We didn't have time for all the fuss at the hotel and were eager to make the most of our time in Istanbul. We set off in search of the Blue Mosque and were overwhelmed by the sight of the most beautiful building we had ever seen. It was adorned with beautiful tiles and elaborate Arabic writing, and the sounds of the call to prayer added to the sense of being in the exotic East. The next day, we took a boat trip that turned into an adventure. Initially, our plan was to take a boat on the Bosporus Sea and get off at an island, but we missed the island and ended up in a place called Yalova. It truly was a beautiful town, and we quickly forgot about missing our stop. We explored this part of the city for a while and eventually got chatting to a local guy in a cafe. He gave us directions for an easier way back to our hotel, involving a train and another boat trip. I'm not sure if it was easier, as it seemed to take some time, but we eventually ended up at the famous Pudding Shop. Back then, it was the meeting place for travellers and hippies on the road to India and beyond. We still didn't have visas for Iran, so we had to spend our final day in Istanbul trying to get them. However, when we got to the Iranian Consulate, they were not processing any more visa applications that day because it was Friday and they closed early. It was just our luck, so we had no choice but to move on and try to get our visas further on in Turkey.

Istanbul

We had a brief stop at Ankara, a modern city where we only had time for a meal before moving on to our next destination, Goreme Valley in the Cappadocia region of Turkey. Goreme was a surprise addition to our trip as it was not on our original itinerary, but we were happy with the diversion. Goreme Valley is located among the "fairy chimney" rock formations. Homes, pigeon houses, and cave churches are carved into the rock. It is not exactly known when Goreme was first inhabited, but it is known that there was a settlement there during the Hittite era between 1800 and 1200 BC. For many centuries, the location was central between rival empires, such as the Hurri-Mitanni, Hittite Empire, Middle Assyrian Empire, Neo-Assyrian Empire, Persian Achaemenid Empire, and the Greek Seleucid Empire. This led the natives to tunnel into the rock to escape the political turmoil. During the Roman era, the area became home to Christians retreating from Rome. Christianity prevailed as the primary religion in the region, which is evident from the many rock churches that still exist there. We visited the honeycombed underground city. Just as we were about to enter, the electricity went off, so we had to use candles to navigate our way through the tunnels. It was a labyrinth of passages and rock formations inside, and the candlelight created strange shadows. The underground city consisted of four floors, but with limited lighting, we could only visit three. Even then, it was a bit nerve-wracking for those with claustrophobia, as at one stage, the passage became so tiny that we had to crawl on all fours to get through.

Goreme was an fascinating place. One day, while out walking, we came across a giant tortoise just waddling along. It was also a paradise of exotic sights, with apple and orange trees and hazelnuts growing abundantly. The women in this region dressed in very colourful clothing, unlike the Northern region of Turkey, where veils were more common. In fact, it almost felt like a different country altogether. The people in this part of Turkey appeared happy, laughing, and joking with each other as they played with the children.

From Goreme, we headed east towards Sivas, where the landscape became more desert-like and barren. Our next overnight stop was Erzurum. It was a grim and dull place, mostly populated by soldiers. It was no surprise to learn that most people preferred to move on from there quickly. There were very few women around, and those we did see were veiled from head to toe, hurrying about their business. During this part of the journey, the females on the bus felt uncomfortable due to the locals' staring, especially in Eastern Turkey. Every time we got off the bus, we were glared at. We all started to wear longer dresses or trousers and long-sleeved tops, and put away the shorts, T-shirts, and vests for another time. We were happy not to extend our stay in Erzurum; it was an uninteresting place and not very welcoming. We continued on to Dogubayazit, towards the Iranian border. On the way, we had a magnificent view of the snow-capped Mount Ararat, standing at approximately 16,814 ft. It is described in the Bible as the resting place of Noah's Ark and is considered to be a sacred mountain by Armenians, as it borders Turkey and Iran. We drove over the Tierre Pass into Iran, and it was very muddy. At one point, everyone had to get off the bus and try to push it! Our old bus was sliding in the mud. It was here that we came across the Bradford to Lahore bus again. As it shot past us at high speed, the passengers cheered. However, when we got further up the pass, we saw that the cheering passengers were now screaming!

The bus had turned over on a bend and toppled over the edge of a cliff. A few other buses met the same fate on this treacherous road, which was very narrow at points with a sheer drop on the other side. There was enough room for only one bus at a time, but cars and buses raced each other to get ahead, so inevitably some were unlucky and went over. Our old bus made it over the pass and reached the Iranian border with everyone intact, albeit muddy and equally muddy passengers. We never saw the *Bradford to Lahore* bus again.

Paul has a bus break in Eastern Turkey

Into Iran

Tabriz was our first stop in Iran. Everyone hopped off the bus to find accommodation. It was just our luck to find the seediest joint in town with an equally seedy owner, as we found out later. The hotel manager was lucky to have his nose intact after our stay there! Just as we settled to go to bed, we saw him looking through a window above our door. Paul gave the door a bang, and our peeping Tom jumped off the ladder, making a lot of noise as he scrambled into the night. We didn't get to see Tabriz as we arrived late in the evening and departed early the next day.

Azadi Tower, Tehran, Iran

At the time of our visit, Iran was ruled by the Shah, who was essentially installed as the ruler of the country by a CIA coup. The Shah wanted to embrace Western values and forsake religion for capitalism. Unfortunately, the speed of change taking place unsettled the Iranians; they had other plans. We were staying a few days in Tehran, which was a modern, noisy city caused by huge traffic jams, hooting horns, and drivers ignoring traffic lights. It reminded me of Istanbul. Crossing a road was dangerous because the lights would be red for cars to stop, but they didn't, so you would have to run the gauntlet.

Surprisingly, the majority of women in Tehran did not wear the burka, especially the younger ones. They wore makeup and Western clothes; they loved Western clothes. The influence of the West was alive and kicking in Tehran, and the young kids liked fashion and the material stuff that came with it. Shahyad Tower, the Shah's Memorial Tower (renamed the Azadi Tower following the 1979 Revolution), standing at 45 metres tall, dominated Tehran and was the gateway to the city. I remember standing beneath it, thinking it was quite ugly. On the plus side of this Western progress was an excellent campsite we stayed at just outside Tehran. It was surprisingly modern with a swimming pool, loungers, hot showers, laundry, and a shop. I got a little over excited and washed all our Levi jeans at the same time. I managed to save one pair earlier in the day, but when I returned later, the other three had disappeared. I later learned that Levi's were valuable in Iran because they were difficult to find, in demand, and they were expensive to buy there. We had to buy local baggy cotton draw-string trousers to replace them, not very fashionable but light and ideal for travelling and better than nothing.

Three women left the bus in Tehran; they were taking up jobs to teach English there. They had borrowed money from one of the other passengers on our bus earlier on the trip and agreed to repay him in Tehran. When he called to where they were living in Tehran, they wouldn't open the door. He never saw them or his money again. It struck me as a weird thing to do, as we had been travelling together for over 3 weeks by the time we got to Tehran. We took off on our own to explore and visited the Tehran Museum, which was not that interesting, and it was also very hot. We were not used to the heat, and walking for an hour or so was tiring. We returned to the campsite to relax and enjoy the fun there by the pool, soaking up the sunshine. It was nice to get a break away from the bus for a few days. At this point, we were now halfway through our journey to Delhi.

Mount Ararat, Eastern Turkey

Travelling towards Mashhad took us through a featureless plain but was worth the journey, as Mashhad was a beautiful city tucked away in northeastern Iran. It is a place of religious pilgrimage and Iran's most sacred city. The name translates to "Place of Martyrdom." A direct descendant of Mohammed was interred here in AD 817; he was the 8th Shi'ite imam, Reza, which explains its importance to the Iranian people. In fact, the first thing you see on arrival to this wonderful city is the great Golden Dome of the Holy Shrine of Imam Reza. By area, it is one of the largest mosques in the world. It was magnificent. Unfortunately, non-Muslims were not allowed inside, but the exterior of the shrine was spectacular, and we settled for that alone.

We explored Mashhad as much as time allowed and found it to be a wonderful, friendly city. We checked into another luxury campsite, again with a pool and great facilities. Iran was full of surprises. Also, on this visit, we had to get our paperwork organised and obtain visas for Afghanistan here. We were excited about this because it was taking us closer to one of the highlights of our trip. After a few hours of queuing, we got our visas. It was a nice big stamp that covered the page of my passport. We became friends with a baker near the campsite. One day, he brought us into the bakery to show us how he made the bread in the traditional way. The bread went through rigorous kneading and was then placed in stone ovens in the wall. It was delicious. After a few days in Mashhad, we were back on the bus heading for the Afghan border.

Afghanistan
Happy Herat — Batty Kandahar — Bustling Kabul —
Jalalabad — up and over the Khyber Pass into Pakistan

We crossed the border from Iran into Afghanistan at Islam Qala-Doug Haroun. The Afghan customs office was a single-story white-painted building. Two turbaned Afghans sat in an office at a long table. We sat on one side, and they sat across from us. They greeted us with "Welcome to Afghanistan" and everyone. They just wanted to chat, and after some time, one of them said, "Ah, Ireland, IRA, bang bang!" We weren't sure what to say or do, but they laughed, so we laughed too. Too scared to do anything else! They carried rifles, and although not scary-looking, we had heard stories and were very careful about what we said and did. Once all the formalities were taken care of, the stamps and more paperwork, we were on our way to Herat. From Herat eastwards lies the only real road in the country, which is Highway 1 naturally! Skirting from Herat around the central spine of the Hindu Kush mountains through the deserts in the south of the country, to Kandahar,

Ghazni, and on to the capital, Kabul. Beyond Kabul, it carries on northwards over the Hindu Kush Mountain range. Our hotel in Herat was called the Mohmand Hotel; it was basic but a welcoming place and perfect for our few days in Herat. We shared a spacious room with three others from the bus, and within minutes of arrival, we had everything we needed for our stay. The Afghans were very friendly and welcoming. The Afghan men were tall and handsome; they were dressed in the traditional way, wearing the Lungee, which is a turban worn differently depending on the region. The Pashtuns wear the Lungee made from good quality cloth to 'signify status. The people from the north of Afghanistan, e.g., the Tajik and the Turkic, wear the Karakul hat, which is made from the wool of sheep. The men wear the Perahan tunban, which is a loose shirt and pants. Women generally wore the burqa and were covered from head to toe, ankles were all that was visible. For formal occasions, they would wear beautiful dresses of vibrant colours with sequins, small tassels, and miniature mirrors sewn into the embroidery. Alcohol was forbidden, and the penalty for being caught drinking alcohol was prison or 60 lashes with a whip. There was little available, and besides, we were risking neither. Men could have up to four wives; they must provide for them, of course. I had wondered why some men had a troupe of veiled women scurrying behind them. They must have been very wealthy.

Outside, the streets were lively. For a tour of the city, you could rent a horse and buggy and trot around at a leisurely pace, taking in the local buzz. They were brightly decorated with spectacular colourful tassels and headgear on the horses, and bells jingled as they trotted about. Trucks were also hand-painted in bright elaborate colours and lights. In the evening, you could hear the bells ringing outside in the street from the horses going around town, as well as the regular call to prayer from the mosque every day, and we got used to these sounds ringing out daily. Herat was home to The Great Mosque of Herat in the city of Herat, Herat Province of northwestern Afghanistan. Built by the Ghurids, under the rule of Sultan Ghiyath al-Din Muhammad Ghori, who laid its foundation in 1200 CE, and later extended by several rulers as Herat changed rulers down the centuries from the Timurids to the Safavids, Mughals, and then the Uzbeks, all of whom supported the mosque. Though many of the glazed tiles have been replaced during subsequent periods, the Friday Mosque in Herat was given its present form during the closing years of the fifteenth century. Apart from the numerous small neighbouring mosques for daily prayer, most communities in the Islamic world have a larger mosque, a congregational mosque for Friday services with a sermon.

The Jama Masjid was not always the largest mosque in Herat; a much larger complex, the Mosque and Madrassa of Gawhar Shad, also built by the Timurids, was located in the northern part of the city. However, it was blown up by British Indian Army officers in 1885 to prevent its use as a fortress if the Russians tried to invade India.

Herat is full of ancient buildings to explore, and the narrow alleyways made it such an interesting labyrinth of wonder. Herat was littered with shops and market stalls selling all sorts of local handicrafts, including Afghan coats and colourful embroidered dresses, tops, and bags, jewellery, and rugs. It wasn't long before I found myself back at the marketplace, bargaining again, this time for a dress. I did buy this time and came away with a beautiful dress. I guessed that I paid too much but enjoyed the banter with the Afghans. The dress was a mix of rich vibrant red colours with sequins and little mirrors sewn into a panel on the front. That transaction took about 2 hours, as everything happens very slowly in Afghanistan, and one had to be very patient. Later that day, a group of us from the bus went along to a place called Kohi-Noor; it was laid on just for tourists. We sat on big cushions on the floor, listened to a group of Afghan musicians, and enjoyed some local dishes of steamed rice and vegetables. It was a nice evening. One day in Herat, myself and Sidney went to the local market, and we were chased out of one market stall because Sidney's shorts were too short.

A shopkeeper in Herat one day was trying to hang a canopy outside his shop, but his lasso skills were not particularly good, and the rope kept getting stuck each time he looped it over the wooden frame. He was also quite old. Sidney jumped to the rescue and climbed the frame like a spider. The shopkeeper threw him the rope, and in no time, the canopy was in place. In the meantime, an audience had gathered below and cheered Sidney as he jumped down. Simple trivial things made them laugh and cheer. I think they found us an amusing bunch of tourists.

Herat, Afghanistan

Sadly, we had to leave Herat, but we left with some great memories of this part of the journey. We still had much more to see in Afghanistan, and so it was decided that we have an early night in readiness for the journey onwards. We had an early start for Kandahar the next day, driving on a straight road through the desert. Dotted around the landscape were caravans of nomadic tents in the distance. These were the Kuchi people, on the move with their families, including livestock such as sheep and goats. The meat, dairy products, hair, and wool from the animals would be exchanged or sold so that the families could purchase grain, vegetables, fruit, and other products of settled life. On the way to Kandahar, a group of people had gathered in the road where earlier a child was fatally knocked down, and our bus was pulled aside at the next village while the tires were inspected for traces of blood. They tried to put the blame on our bus, and after two hours, we were finally allowed to go on. It would have been impossible for our bus to hit the child as we were too far away when the incident happened. About half an hour later, we were pulled over again while the bus was inspected by local police, again checking the tires for any signs of blood. They found nothing, and again we could go on. It was scary too because we weren't sure how the whole situation would work out. Our driver had done this journey many times and told us that it happens regularly as they see it as a way of getting insurance money from foreigners. We finally reached Kandahar later that day. I remember one night I was at a food stall, and bats were everywhere, just flitting past my head, getting very close to touching it. It was strange because I had never seen bats outside a zoo. Here, they were just flying about.

We spent just one night in Kandahar and left the next day for Kabul. It was a superb journey over the Kabul pass, and we were looking forward to a 3-night stay in Kabul with a comfortable bed and a decent meal to sit down to. Kabul was a big surprise; it was a modern and commercial city, bustling with shops and colourful stalls mainly selling hippy clothing and jewellery and of course Afghan coats. Kabul was very much like Herat but on a grander scale. The hotel was not great, but we were not disappointed as we had by now got used to the unexpected. It was cheap but not cheerful. One night didn't hurt, and we found a better one for the remaining two nights. I enjoyed bartering with a local tribesman, swapping a Casio watch for a Yak wool jumper and socks in Kabul, which came in handy for our return journey in mid-winter.

Outside clothes shop Chicken Street, Kabul

Afghani Trucks and Drivers on the road

On the Khyber Pass

Into Pakistan

From Kabul, we travelled on the national highway through the Kabul Gorge, a breathtaking and nerve-wracking, treacherous, bendy road into Pakistan. The gorge, in some places, is no more than a few hundred yards wide and is framed by vertical rock cliffs that soar more than 2,000 feet above the Kabul River below. It is a two-lane highway with barely enough room for two cars to pass, and it has been the scene of many accidents. Cars raced each other to get ahead first. It was possibly more spectacular than the Khyber Pass into Peshawar. On the way, we had to camp out as there were no places to stay in this remote area. During the night, we experienced the most incredible electric storm, with very loud thunder followed by bolts of lightning. The sky turned a strange shade of yellow, and everyone abandoned their tents and ran for cover under or in the bus. Some of the tents were torn to shreds in the wind. The next morning, everyone went out to see what was left of their belongings. We found our tent still pitched with little or no damage. Once everyone had their belongings together again, we drove on to Lahore, arriving there in the evening. Lahore was not a very friendly place, and the one night we stayed was mostly spent inside the hotel, emerging only to go for a meal in a local café with a couple of people from our bus. While we were waiting for our meal at the café, a tall man with long black hair and a beard appeared at the door and stared straight at us. When he realised I was looking at him, he stuck his tongue out at me. It was a weird experience, but that was our welcome to Lahore! Later that night, rattan beds appeared on the street, and a local guy told us that people rent them because they have nowhere to live. It was like a large outdoor dormitory with no place to wash or use a toilet. Men, women, and children simply slept on their wooden carts, which they used for their work. In Pakistan, for some people, their wooden cart was all they possessed. They worked with it and slept on it. It was the first time we had seen such poverty.

The drive from Pakistan into India was through similar terrain, but the atmosphere changed once we crossed the border into India. The noticeable difference was the sheer number of people; it was bustling. We had both looked forward to our arrival in India. We had our passports stamped at the border and headed to Amritsar in the Indian state of Punjab, home to the Sikh Golden Temple with its distinctive copper dome. It is a chief pilgrimage destination for Sikhs from all over the world. There are guest houses on the site and a huge dining hall that provides meals for the thousands of pilgrims arriving each day. Once in Amritsar, we wasted no time and took a rickshaw straight to the Golden Temple. We were met by a Sikh guide who gave us a tour of the temple, explaining its history. For me, it was probably the most stunning building I had ever entered. The temple itself is erected on an island surrounded by a sacred pool. Our guide told us about the history of the holy books and the holy men at the temple who read the sacred scriptures. It was a mesmerising place with a deep sense of peace and tranquillity. I felt humbled there. Walking around the temple, I remember feeling as if I had stepped back in time, with holy men wearing long robes bent over giant books in alcoves overlooking the sacred pool. It truly was a very humbling experience. We had a meal there, and the guide invited us to stay overnight. We didn't stay but vowed to return again one day. It was our first real taste of India, and we were not disappointed, simply curious to see more.

Arrival in Delhi and Departure From Our Friends

Our final leg of the journey was to take us to Delhi. This particular day involved a lot of driving, and we had to keep moving with few stops in order to arrive there before dark. I fell fast asleep for a long time. The motion of the bus would often send you into a deep sleep. Seng woke me up to tell me we had arrived in Delhi. I looked out the window and saw that just about every mode of transport was teeming around the city: rickshaws, bicycles, cars, trucks, and traffic police with sticks hitting errant drivers as they passed. It was chaotic, but unbelievably, the traffic kept moving. Evan was taking us to a campsite outside of the city to park the bus. By now, we had become good friends with Evan and Bill, the drivers. They had covered the route to India for over 10 years and knew what to expect along the way, although sometimes the unexpected happened. Our fellow travellers were from Malaysia, Australia, America, Canada, England, Scotland, and us, the only Irish passengers. We had become good friends with Seng from Malaysia, Hugo from Canada, Noel from Scotland, Trevor from Birmingham, and Sidney from Somerset, and we swapped addresses before we left the bus. Evan came down with a bug when we arrived in Delhi, and we decided to wait with him until his wife arrived from London. After a few days, we set off on our own adventure.

We took a rickshaw into Delhi to have a look around and to get our visas for Nepal. It was so hot that we were melting, but we had to get our visas sorted out and buy some food. We were on our own from now on, and the real adventure began. We had all been like a little family on the bus for six weeks, and without knowing it, we knew that we had each other to comfort us in anxious times. A few days after we left the bus, while we were visiting the Red Fort in Delhi, we whizzed past a traffic island on a rickshaw and there was James and Mona, looking lost in the middle of it! I hoped they found a way to cross the street from there. Each mode of transport moved at speed and at times getting into a rickshaw was risky. For us, it was still early days, and once we got used to the chaos in the cities, it was more than compensated for when we stayed in more tranquil villages in India.

We found the bus station and got tickets for Rishikesh, our next destination for the following day. I found a bookshop in Old Delhi and bought Bram Stoker's Dracula. Every time I turned a page, it fell out. By the time I finished the book, the pages were detached from the cover! It was a bumpy ride to Rishikesh. When we finally got there, we found a chai house and got chatting to a guy who directed us to Swiss Cottage for cheap accommodation. It was a wonderful place, a house with a big garden run by a Swami for budget travellers like us. However, he had no rooms available, so he allowed us to camp in the gardens until a room was free. But first, we had to join him for tea. He had an open fire with a hook hanging over it for the kettle. It took about an hour for the tea to be ready! This is how things were in India, and we got used to everything happening very slowly. We pitched the tent in the lovely garden with amazing views of the mountains. We were completely unaware that there were some slithery campers there too, but they never troubled us.

Swiss Cottage, Rishikesh, India

Our stay in Rishikesh went from one week to two weeks; it was hard to leave. During our stay, we visited a yoga retreat, which entailed crossing a river in a small boat. I had seen an old travelling lady earlier on the shore, and now she was in the boat with snakes wrapped up in a shawl. I could see them wriggling in the cloth. She opened the cloth to set them free on the boat, but the boatman told her to put them back. The boat trip was short, and suddenly, we had a friend to take us to the yoga retreat. He wore just a loincloth around his waist and carried a stick. Not sure what the stick was for, but probably stray dogs as there were a lot of them about! He called himself Monkey Man. He seemed to drift into our lives from nowhere. He took on the role of a guardian angel and looked out for us, making sure nobody ripped us off. He took us to his village to meet his family and have tea and chapatis. The ashram was already in full flow with a yoga class, and I really couldn't see myself joining in. I was put off by the number of Westerners wearing orange robes and loincloths, trying to go native and be cool! It was funny. There was never any doubt in my mind that Rishikesh was an incredibly special place, not just because the Beatles had visited back in the '60s, but because it was such a lively place with something always happening. It was full of yoga teachers and healers. We found a tailor in a street near Swiss Cottage. He had a small stall and a sewing machine. We chose some cotton material and asked him to make shirts and trousers for us. We needed light cotton clothes for the Indian climate. It was a great novelty to have clothes made to measure.

On the Nepalese border with local children

After a few weeks, we decided it was time to move on to Nepal, travelling by train to Lucknow and then on to Gorakhpur. It was a long and tedious journey, packed both inside and outside. Passengers travelled on the roof of the trains in India with huge cloth bundles of belongings. By now, we were fed up with being asked the same questions over and over again. The most common question was whether we were married, how many children we had, and if we had none, why not! Most of the time, we pretended to be asleep or spoke in Irish. We were on the move into Nepal and the Himalayas.

We reached the Nepalese border in Raxaul around mid-November. It was busy with buses, taxis, rickshaws, and just about any mode of transport imaginable, with porters to carry bags and buses for onward journeys. It was buzzing. An American guy wearing a cowboy hat offered us a bus ride to Kathmandu for a few dollars. We joined him and the other overlanders who were already on the bus. Our journey to Kathmandu from Raxaul was an incredible one, taking us up through the Himalayas. The road seemed endless as we climbed the winding path with spectacular views. It truly was a magical journey. The overcrowding of India was now a distant memory, replaced by fresh mountain air and banana plantations. It was quieter, calmer, and more peaceful. The bus stopped just outside a small village where we camped for the night under the stars. The cowboy driver played his guitar until we could no longer stay awake. The high altitude made us tire quickly, but after a while, we got used to it. The next morning, we went to the village and had a breakfast of boiled eggs and bananas while monkeys played in the trees above us.

In Pokhara, we found a little cafe, which was always good for checking out accommodation options. We met up with an

Australian guy from the Budget bus, swapped stories, and he introduced us to a house for rent as he was leaving Pokhara. We took the house for a month, and it even included a small flat-bottomed boat called a Dungan on Lake Pokhara.

Lake Pokhara

It was like paradise. The Annapurna Mountain range, including Machhapuchhre and Hiunchuli, kept a watchful eye over Pokhara with their wondrous snow-capped peaks against the clear blue sky. It was a heavenly place to wake up in the morning. The house itself was basic but luxurious compared to camping, which we had grown tired of by this point. It had one large room upstairs and a sitting area downstairs with a dug-out area for cooking. Outside, there was a small veranda, a great spot for sitting and watching the world go by. Every morning, local Nepalese women would come by to sell eggs and mushrooms. They were stunningly beautiful, always giggling and happy. They were also incredibly strong, carrying large baskets of wood up and down the mountains barefoot. The baskets were attached to a headband and straps around their shoulders. They weighed a ton. Paul tried to lift one and could barely move it off the ground. They had a good laugh at this. Sometimes, if they saw that you looked serious or sad, they would stand in front of you and imitate your face. I couldn't help but laugh at that. The language barrier prevented us from having a proper conversation, but we communicated through actions, and they found it all very funny. They were never sad, always smiling and cheerful.

Our home in Pokhara

Our diet in Nepal mainly consisted of omelettes, pancakes, rice, and vegetable dishes. One day, while at the store collecting supplies we bumped into Hugo and Noel from the bus and arranged to meet up for dinner and have a special cake at the cafe. Hugo had met a Swiss girl, and she came along too. We had a lot to talk about since leaving the bus. We decided to try out our small boat and took our guests across the lake. All five of us crammed into the small boat, but unfortunately, it sank not long after we pulled away from the shore. I remember trying to save the camera from the water, and luckily, it did dry out eventually.

Our daily visitors in Pokhara

Some Nepalese men were watching us from the shore and were laughing at us. They disappeared for a short while and arrived with another boat to take us across the lake. By the time we got there, it was getting dark. We ended up staying overnight with a Nepalese family who looked after us well. We sat around a wood-burning fire with the daughters while the others cooked for us and fed us popcorn while we waited for the main dish. They were lovely, welcoming people and giggled a lot. One of the daughters liked Noel and just kept staring at him, maybe it was his red hair; he enjoyed it. The next morning, we rowed back to the shore, and when we all tumbled out of the boat, we all agreed that it was like a dream. We said goodbye to Noel, Hugo, and their friend and headed back to our little house to contemplate our adventure on the lake.

Life was good in Pokhara. Another day we bumped into Trevor and invited him to stay with us for a short while. I wasn't sure what had happened to Trevor since we left the bus in Delhi, but he did seem to be a bit shell-shocked and very thin. He had been buying many things on his journey to take home, including beautiful rugs and local crafts. He was happy to see us again. We noticed he was seldom eating and sleeping a lot. We heard of an event going on in town one day and invited Trevor along. We had no idea that part of the celebrations involved a goat being sacrificed at it was shocking to witness. Trevor was physically sick at the sight of it. He had become a vegetarian and Buddhist during his journey to India. We were unaware of this, but after that day, he became more withdrawn and would eat very little. One day we returned from the shop and found him giving away everything to our Nepalese neighbours through the upstairs window. Trevor then exposed all his film from his trip and gave away his camera. We decided to give up the house, and if we left, Trevor would more than likely leave too. He was becoming so withdrawn that we were worried for him. It was difficult to leave Pokhara because it was like paradise. The landscape, the mountains, and its people were beautiful in every way. It is a place that will always be in my heart. Trevor then decided it was time to go back to the UK. Trevor finally realised that he was unwell and needed to go back to the UK, We travelled with him to the airport and then made our way to Kathmandu to stay a few days.

Kathmandu was full of life, colourful and noisy, but not in a bad way, but noticeable after the tranquillity of Pokhara.

This time we had a chance to check out the sights, including the Living Goddess who lives in the Kumari's house. She represents the Goddess Kumari and is worshipped with great reverence.

Swayambhunagh Monkey Temple, Kathmandu

She is chosen from several young candidates from the Shakya caste from the Newars; some are only four years of age. They must pass an extremely strict and harrowing selection process to obtain the title. She must remain calm and show no signs of fear even when being put through some scary tests. Her feet must never touch the ground, and she can only leave the residence during certain festivals. She will remain the Living Goddess until she reaches puberty. We found a great little place called 'Hotch Potch,' which was not too far from the centre and a short walk to Swayambhunath. Its nickname is the Monkey Temple because Swayambhunath was a bit of a tongue twister for European visitors. It is the holiest Buddhist stupa in Nepal. The monkeys run around freely here but are harmless. There are numerous shrines and monasteries on its premises. Kathmandu was less populated than the Indian cities. We stayed in Kathmandu for four days and then began our journey south. Our visas were running out, and it was beginning to get quite cold in Nepal. Kathmandu seemed less populated than the Indian cities, but still many people milling around and many beggars without limbs on the streets. We stayed in Kathmandu for four days and then began our journey south. Our visas were about to expire, and it was beginning to get cold in Nepal. Our next leg of the journey was to be an incredible one down to the Nepalese town of Birgunj and crossing the border at Raxaul, which is one of the northernmost towns in the Indian state of Bihar. It is right near the border between India and Nepal. The town is located near the Sariswa and Bangari Rivers and is a busy border crossing between Nepal and India. The journey itself truly was the most scenic trip I have ever been on. We could see Mount Everest, and the freshness of the air and clear blue skies were exhilarating. We reached Birgunj in the evening and enjoyed a welcome meal. By now, we were eating curry for breakfast, lunch, and dinner. When we got to Raxaul, we found a little place to stay and enjoyed the evenings when we would sit at the Chai shops just watching the world go by and the locals gossiping in Hindi. Our hotel was not up to much; it was called the De Luxe Hotel, but there was nothing deluxe about it. It suited us for the brief time we were there. We got a bus to Muzaffarpur and then on to Sonpur in the Bihar region of India. Sonpur was once famous for having the longest railway platform. From here we would take the train to Varanasi. An Indian family we had gotten friendly with here arranged for us to travel in style with a sleeper, and we shared the compartment with them. They shared their homemade food, which was delicious – rice, dahl, chapatis, and chai. They were extremely organised with pots that were layered to divide the different dishes, plates, and cups. We were now dining in style. We would normally be hopping on and off the train at stops to buy snacks from food stalls, not on this journey.

Arrival in Benares was absolute chaos; everyone spilled off the train all at once, and the station was teeming with people. We pushed our way through the crowds to find the exit and eventually spilled out onto the street into the heat and dust.

Varanasi (also known as Benares) is an incredible city on the banks of the River Ganges. It is a major hub for Hindu and Jain faiths. Hindus believe that dying and cremation along the banks of the holy Ganges River allows one to break the cycle of rebirth and attain salvation, making it a major centre for pilgrims. The city is known worldwide for its many ghats, embankments made in steps of stone slabs along the riverbank, where pilgrims perform ritual ablutions. Of particular note are the Dashashwamedh Ghat, the Panchganga Ghat, the Manikarnika Ghat, and the Harishchandra Ghat, the last two being where Hindus cremate their dead. The River Ganges flows through India and Bangladesh.

Varanasi was an overcrowded, noisy city, and I wasn't prepared for it. It was more noticeable because we had just come from a very tranquil place and had gotten used to the peace and quiet. A rickshaw took us to Sarnath, approximately 10 km from Varanasi. It was at Sarnath that Lord Buddha founded Buddhism in 528 BCE when he made his first sermon there. Sarnath was full of Buddhist temples and was a major place of pilgrimage for Buddhists from India and abroad. Several countries in which Buddhism is practised, such as Thailand, Japan, Tibet, Sri Lanka, and Myanmar, established temples and monasteries in Sarnath in the style typical of their respective countries. In Sarnath, it was possible to have a basic room at the Buddhist monastery in return for a small donation. The monastery was run by the Mahabodhi Society. We settled into life at Sarnath for a while and visited many temples during our time there. The Buddhist monks would be up early in the morning, chanting and saying their mantras. It was a very calm place for us after travelling by bus and train for so long. In the evening, it was a beautiful, peaceful place to walk and feel the cool air as the sun went down. It was a perfect retreat after the long bus and train journeys. Sarnath was nice and peaceful.

One day, we decided to brave it and return to Varanasi. It was packed with rickshaws, motorbikes, cars, cows, bicycles milling around, and people bathing and washing on the riverbank, while further on, the bodies were lined up ready for cremation, with their ashes put into the Ganges. Old men sat by the riverbank with umbrellas to shade them from the stifling heat. There were circus acts going on all over the city, troupes of people bending iron rods, throwing knives, swallowing fire, and walking over hot ashes in their bare feet just to make some money. The whole city buzzed with activity. I was shocked at first, but then I got used to it. That's how life was in Benares, but it was nice to return to the peace and tranquillity of Sarnath.

In Benares, we booked our train tickets for Agra and included a sleeper for this journey, which would take us through Allahabad, Gwalior, and then to Agra. The train carriages were absolutely packed with people, and some were even travelling on the roof of the train. Every possible space on the train was taken, and if you moved to get comfortable in your seat, someone would squeeze in beside you. In the chaos, vendors passed through the carriage selling sweets or samosas. I have no idea how they did this every day without being injured or crushed to death. There was a toilet on the train, but it was an ordeal to get there and best avoided if possible. The Indian passengers asked us the same questions throughout the journey, and although we answered politely, we sometimes spoke Irish to each other since they didn't understand our foreign language. "A feeling of relief" is an understatement as we pulled into Agra. We were mentally exhausted and needed air and space after the crowded train. We found a wonderful place to stay and made our way to the Taj Mahal the next day. It was stunning, possibly the most spectacular building I had ever seen.

One day, we met Mr Moghul at Moghul Jewels. He presented us with some beautiful stones, but our budget was so tight that we couldn't buy them. However, we had a camera that Mr Moghul took a fancy to, and we did a swap. Mr Moghul was pleased with his new camera, and we went away with precious stones and some cotton tops.

The cold finally drove us further south towards Bombay (now Mumbai) via Jaipur. It was a long journey, and we developed a love-hate relationship with the Indian trains. At Bombay railway station, a French guy in a loincloth was begging. He had a badly infected leg and claimed the money was for a doctor. I doubted that he would use the money for medical treatment, but I gave him £10. There were so many beggars at the railway stations that it was impossible to give everyone money, but they saw us as rich. The original plan had been to stay in Bombay, but it was too noisy and dirty, so we decided to head straight for Goa.

Eventually, we left Bombay by boat to Goa. The boat trip was cheap and included lunch for both of us, but it was an awful journey, and I was ill for most of it, unable to eat or sit up to enjoy the scenery.

The boat was headed to Panjim (now known as Panaji), which was a beautiful city and the capital of Goa. The Christian influence in Panjim came from its Portuguese ancestry, evident in its typical Portuguese-influenced architecture. We arrived in Panjim in the early hours of the morning and found the bus stop to take us to Colva beach. The journey to Colva was wonderful, taking us through lush green scenery and palm trees, creating a tropical atmosphere. When we got off the bus, the heat was so intense that we had to quickly seek shade under a palm tree. While it was possible to rent palm leaf huts on the beach at Colva, we opted to find our own spot further up the beach and pitched our tent. Due to the scorching sun, we added an extension canopy to provide shade from the heat. We had people dropping by every day for chai, and we soon got to know many of the local restaurant owners and other Westerners staying in the beach huts. We formed a little community. The local restaurant, Caroline's, was a great spot. After everyone finished eating, the tables and chairs would be rearranged to make room for dancing. Bob Marley's music would play, and everyone would take to the dance floor at Caroline's on the beach. We also had breakfast there, and it became our dining room during our stay in Goa. Caroline, along with her family of six, ran this fantastic place.

Christmas was approaching, and the Christian influence in this part of India was on full display. Everyone dressed up in colourful clothing, and the celebrations went on for days. The cakes created were like works of art, coming in all shapes and sizes, although they were so sweet, they bordered on being bitter. It felt like an endless celebration.

Homeward Bound

As the weeks drifted by, so did our cash, and the decision to start the journey home, although difficult, was now necessary. We knew that the journey back would be unpredictable because we would be relying on local buses, trains, and hitchhiking where it felt safe to do so. We were down to about $150, which was not a lot considering we had a journey of 6,000 miles ahead of us. We had no idea what we were taking on, but we were homeward bound. Little did we know that some days we would have to eat literally nothing so that we could buy a bus or train ticket. There were transit visas to factor in too, so going home on a budget was an understatement.

We booked a train for Delhi with a sleeper so that we would not have to answer the many questions we were usually asked on a train journey in India. It was nice to get a good sleep while travelling through the Indian countryside. A guy on the train started talking to us and recommended a man called Sam in Delhi who provided cheap accommodation. Another recommendation was the Asoka Mission in Mehrauli, run by Buddhist monks, in a neighbourhood south of Delhi. We pulled into Delhi and headed for the Station restaurant. The food there was remarkably good and cheap. The city train station restaurants were great, and the waiters wore black trousers with white shirts, and some even wore white gloves, which was funny. The menu at the station restaurants was varied and included scrambled eggs. It was a pleasant change from rice, curry, and samosas for months. We ordered our breakfast and relaxed at the station, watching the world go by. It was always mad busy with people moving huge bags, bundles of blankets, boxes—anything. In the middle of it all, stray dogs wandered around the platforms looking for scraps of food or fighting with each other.

We made our way to the Asoka Mission in Mehrauli, which was run by Buddhist monks. We stayed one night; it was ridiculously cheap but by no means cheerful. It was also full of Western junkies strung out on heroin or anything they could lay their hands on. They were like the living dead, walking around out of their heads and unwell. One day, we saw a well-fed Buddhist monk smoking a big cigar in the middle of all the chaos—it looked like an odd situation. Some travellers to India really did lose their way; I saw that not just now but many times earlier on in our trip. One night was enough in this place, after which we checked out and found Sam's place.

Sam was a great guy. He spoke really good English, very loudly, but he was a nice, friendly guy and welcomed us to his place. The accommodation comprised a big dormitory-type room on the roof of the house. Sam and his wife slept in the dorm too, only their "room" was separated by a blanket hanging on a clothesline. It was a clean and quiet place; with a shower I could never forget. The shower comprised two wooden panels—you stepped in and a person outside could pour a bucket of warm (sometimes cold) water over the door. It was simple and funny at the time, but it worked. The beds were made from wood and rattan and very squeaky. At night, we would giggle at hearing Sam and his wife's bed creaking. On the way back to Sam's one night, we met a devotee of the Children of God who was asking for money to help Western prisoners in Delhi. We gave him 10 rupees, and then he asked us if we would like to come to the house for dinner that evening. We had nothing else to do, so we said yes, we'd love to—or so we thought at the time!

He gave us the address, and we were surprised at the lovely house we were invited to. It was in a nice part of Delhi and had tall ceilings, with a strong smell of incense burning as we walked through the door. The people there were very friendly. They were a nice group of people, all Westerners, and they made a beautiful meal followed by music played on their guitars, tambourines, and bongos, and they sang. It was very pleasant. As they were a religious group, after the food and music, we had to stay for the sermon from the Elder of the group, which essentially spoke about the evil West and how bad it would be for all present to return to their Western lives and abandon the East. The East was where we should be, etc. We didn't feel like that at all. We could make a good living in the West and had options that I perhaps would not have out East. This was our adventure to the East, just to experience the different cultures here, but not to live there forever. We finally became uncomfortable with the whole situation, and it seemed that we would not be able to get out of the house in the normal fashion, i.e., out the front door. So, we hatched a plan: I went first to the bathroom on the ground floor and escaped out the toilet window! Paul followed a few minutes later. Phew! We were relieved to get away and vowed not to get into any sticky situations and decline any further dinner invitations.

We got our visas for the return journey through Iran before we left Delhi but had to take one final rickshaw ride to the old city and had a wonderful time taking in the chaos once more before we said goodbye. I almost felt a bit sad to be leaving. So much had happened in a short space of time; I felt I would never be the same again.

It was time to get moving, so we made our way to Amritsar again, staying only one night because we were now on a mission to move as fast as possible west—cash was running out. It was getting colder this time around in Amritsar. From there, we would travel to Peshawar and then to Lahore, where we stayed in a guest house with a bull in the yard! Not a guard dog, but a bull! The quickest way to Quetta was by train, and from there, we would take the train to Zahedan in Iran. This would take us into Balochistan, which is tucked in between Pakistan and Iran. It was a tribal region. Soldiers rode on the train with rifles, as the region had trouble with bandits attacking the train in the past. The 36-hour train journey to Zahedan took 6 days. Our original plan had been to go back through Afghanistan, but severe weather and the need to buy another visa made us change our plans and head to Quetta. That way, we could bypass Afghanistan altogether.

On the train to Quetta, we met a French guy and decided to get a triple room at a hotel to save money on accommodation. Our hotel was sleazy, with an even sleazier proprietor. When we settled into the room, the French guy produced a joint and began to smoke it. After about 5 minutes, our room was full of Pakistani police. It was probably the scariest thing I have ever experienced. During the 1970s, the penalties for being found in possession of drugs in Pakistan were very serious. We had heard many stories of Westerners being locked up, and money being the only way to secure their release. Our bags were thoroughly searched, even the frame bars of our rucksacks. Naturally, we were worried, as we had gone out earlier for a meal, and the door to our room could not be properly locked. It occurred to me that drugs might have been planted in our luggage. Finally, the local police left the room, and we were relieved. The French guy lit another joint, and I asked him to get rid of it. We had come this far and did not want any hassle from authorities, especially with drugs. We had a rule not to carry anything like that for ourselves or anyone else. It was too risky. Five minutes later, there was another knock at the door, and the general police came in. The same search commenced. They asked us how much money we had and for our passports. When they saw our Irish passports, they realised we were not the group of three they were looking for. The hotel owner had been tipped off that three French travellers were carrying drugs. He had assumed it was us because of the French guy with us. Sleazy lived up to his name. We parted company with the French guy the next morning. He was a liability and best left to travel alone.

The next day, it was snowing and absolutely freezing cold. It was now mid-February. My Afghan jumper and socks, which I had traded for my watch earlier in the trip, came in very handy for the bitter cold weather.

When we arrived at the station and went to board the train, I was told that females had to travel in the last carriage, reserved only for women and children. The station master had to go to each carriage alone and ask if we could travel with them. After a little while, we finally got the okay from a group of young men. Two hours later, the train finally started moving out of Quetta. We didn't care about the delay as long as we finally got moving. Nothing ever left or arrived on time, and we learned to accept this over time in the East. The boys in our carriage were a noisy bunch but not unpleasant. I loved their colourful hats. They were very childish in some ways, laughing at silly things, but that may have been due to the amount of weed they smoked every day! The old guy in the carriage snored, and they would imitate his snoring when he was awake. Silly things like that. It was fun sharing the carriage with them because they were also entertaining, plus they saved me from travelling in the cage-like carriage at the end of the train with the women and children. Some older men in the carriage kept to themselves and just observed the antics of the younger ones, but mainly they slept. The train was full of sheep and chickens, and there were parrots in cages too. The sheep were kept in the toilet, so each time anyone needed to use it, the sheep would be taken out and put in the aisle.

The guys in our carriage found this highly amusing, but I did not. They were smuggling blankets from Pakistan into Iran, as we discovered later. Although we had been told the journey would take 36 hours, it took 6 days. On the sixth day, we had enough and left the train, taking a local bus the rest of the way.

Sign language, laughs, and sighs became our means of communication with the people in the carriage, as their English was limited. They could only say 'mister' and 'missus.' We became mister and missus. At the beginning of the journey, the train chugged through the desert and occasionally made stops where food stalls magically appeared, selling basic and cheap items like fruit, boiled eggs, bread, and local dishes served on leaves or newspaper. These stops provided a welcome distraction from the monotonous desert scenery.

Armed soldiers carrying rifles were present on the train due to past incidents involving bandits. It felt like being in a scene from a cowboy film. One day, I spotted a horseman wearing tribal clothing and carrying a rifle. I couldn't help but wonder if he was a bandit or a soldier. The train journey had a surreal and never-ending quality to it.

On one occasion, the train came to a complete halt, and everyone got off to inspect the scene. It turned out that the tracks had been washed away and needed repair. As a result, food on the train ran out, and some passengers resorted to throwing their parrots out of the window, as they had died during the journey. Darkness brought pitch blackness to the carriage, with only occasional torchlights or the glow from the boys' joints providing any illumination.

One day, a small man entered the carriage, and the boy's made music by banging cans and singing. The little man started dancing in the aisles, and they laughed uncontrollably. After he finished dancing, they playfully dangled him out of the window for a few minutes. It was a sight like none other. Despite the language barrier, we developed a camaraderie with the boys, although it was hard to tell if they genuinely liked us or simply tolerated us.

They piled up blankets packed in plastic wrapping one day and offered us a seat on them. Naively, we accepted, only to find ourselves elevated so high that we couldn't see out the window. When we reached the Pakistani-Iranian border Mirjveh, the police boarded the train and confiscated all the blankets. After some negotiation and bribery, the blankets were returned, and we continued our journey.

Eventually, the train reached a point where a bus to Zahedan was waiting. We gladly disembarked, eager to leave the train behind. The bus ride was a welcome change, despite the driver's maniacal speed. We arrived in Zahedan, where we found a good place to eat and tasted the delicious stone-baked bread. To our surprise, the train arrived not long after us, and the boys from the carriage spotted us. They ran up to us clapping and smiling, as if they had found long-lost friends. We felt touched and guilty for wanting to get away from them. We spent some time eating and laughing with them in Zahedan cherishing the bond we had formed. And realising had they not agreed to us travelling in the train carriage back in Quetta we would have missed out on a lot of fun. I felt sad to say goodbye, they shook hands with us and blessed us.

From Zahedan, we took a bus to Tehran and reunited with two English drivers we had previously met in Istanbul. They offered to drive us to Zagreb, Yugoslavia, which would cover a significant distance. We accepted their offer, especially as winter had set in, and we wanted to move through Europe quickly. The journey included crossing the treacherous Tierre Pass, where we faced challenges due to heavy snow and icy conditions. However, we made it through and continued driving through bleak villages in Eastern Turkey, encountering few people apart from soldiers who asked for money and food. We felt safer staying in the truck, which was surprisingly comfortable and modern, equipped with bunk beds.

Upon reaching Istanbul, we said goodbye to the drivers and met another English driver named Mark, who offered to take us from Istanbul to Zagreb. It was a fortunate encounter, as it took us closer to home. Zagreb, however, proved to be a disappointing place, and we quickly hitchhiked out of it, facing harsh weather and limited accommodation options. After walking for miles each day, we finally received a lift from a generous Yugoslavian man heading to Munich. We were immensely grateful to him, as he provided us with food and made the journey more comfortable.

We continued hitchhiking, and eventually, we were picked up by a young man who was travelling all the way to Paris. It was an unbelievable stroke of luck, especially as he spoke perfect English. He even accompanied us to the main post office in Paris, where we picked up our post. The envelope contained the much-awaited cash. We treated ourselves to some delicious French bread, cheese, and coffee, relishing the moment.

Our plans to catch a ferry from Carteret in Northeast France back to Jersey were disrupted by the winter season, forcing us to change our route and head to Boulogne for the ferry to Dover. However, in Brittany, we had a chance encounter that led us to a beautiful chateau with a lake, where we were invited to stay. It provided a much-needed respite, and we enjoyed the warmth of French hospitality, home-cooked meals, and comfortable beds.

Our host arranged a lift for us to Boulogne, ensuring we didn't have to hitchhike anymore in France. The ferry to England and the subsequent journey to Holyhead were straightforward, and it was a relief to set foot on Irish soil again. We took the number 83 bus home to Crumlin, a short distance from Dublin City centre marking the end of our journey in relative style. It was nice to be home.

The hippie trail came to an end in the late 1970s due to various events, including the Iranian Revolution and the invasion of Afghanistan by Russia. These geopolitical changes closed off the overland route to India and beyond. In hindsight, we consider ourselves incredibly fortunate to have travelled through these countries, especially Afghanistan, during a time of relative peace.

Epilogue

When we finally recovered from the culture shock on returning to the Western Hemisphere, we soon realised it was time to find meaningful employment. It also meant we had to settle down again into the nine to five routines for a while at least. On the plus side it was nice to be back among our family and friends, in our warm comfortable beds, eating home cooked meals, hot baths and fresh clean clothes to wear. But the urge for more adventure was very strong and within a year we were on our way back to Jersey and making plans for the next trip.

Unfortunately, I have no photographs of the return part of our journey because I had traded our camera with Mr Mughal in Agra in return for gemstones. It took some weeks to get back to Ireland, in all we had travelled over seven thousand two hundred kilometres by train, bus, hitchhiking (in Europe mainly) and on foot. Our hitchhiking relied on the good nature of all the wonderful people we encountered on the way. Without them I would not be here to write this story.